Murder in the Heather:
The Winter Hill Murder of 1838

by David Holding

First published by
Scott Martin Productions, 2019
www.scottmartinproductions.com

Published in Great Britain in 2019 by
Scott Martin Productions
10 Chester Place,
Adlington, Chorley, PR6 9RP
scottmartinproductions@gmail.com
www.scottmartinproductions.com

Electronic version and paperback versions available
for purchase on Amazon.

All photographs and sketches in this publication are
the author's own, with the exception of the '19th
Century Percussion Lock Fowling Piece' which was
downloaded with thanks from gunseekers.co.uk
(public domain catalogue).

Acknowledgements

It is always difficult to remember when undertaking research of any kind, all the people who It is always difficult to remember when undertaking research of any kind, all the people who helped along the way with advice, encouragement and information. I should like to express my thanks to those who played a pivotal role in bringing my original work from an initial concept to full fruition. To all these people I express my sincere and grateful thanks. My thanks also go to those anonymous but ever helpful staff at the numerous institutions and archives I have consulted. I would wish to single out for special thanks and appreciation the following:

Lancashire County Record Office, Preston.
Bolton Central Reference Library and Local Studies Department.
The Staff at the Harris Library, Preston.
The Staff at Blackburn Reference Library.
The Manchester Metropolitan University Local Studies Department.

Acknowledgement is also paid to members of both the medical and legal professions, for the benefit of their expertise on the various matters raised in this work. My gratitude loses no sincerity in its generality. I would, however, hasten to add that none of the above are responsible for the contents of this work, any mistakes are entirely my own.

David Holding 2019

'Scotsman's Stump'.

North-East Slope of Winter Hill.

Contents

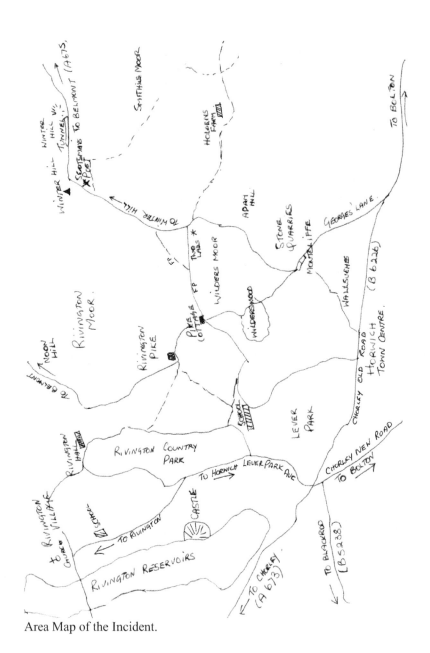

Area Map of the Incident.

Introduction

Winter Hill and nearby Rivington Moor are familiar landmarks to the inhabitants of the neighbouring townships of Horwich and Bolton, lying in the valley below. They present a challenge to the adventurous hiker who, after a struggle to the summit of Winter Hill some 1,475 feet above sea level, will have his or her efforts amply rewarded by the view it affords on a clear day. To the north-east can be seen the slopes of Pendle Hill and further still, the outline of the Yorkshire Dales.

The most direct route covering the area of our case is from Bolton along the B6226 Chorley Old Road, which was formerly the old Turnpike Road from Bolton to Chorley. Just before the road drops down towards Horwich, there is on the left-hand side the 'Jolly Crofters' Inn, and almost directly opposite is Georges Lane. This lane runs along the moor's edge towards Rivington Pike passing several stone quarries. The main working quarry today is at Montcliffe, which was a small hamlet with a colliery and miners' cottages. Bearing right past Montcliffe Quarry, there is a modern road constructed for access to the TV station and radio masts on Winter Hill. This road follows the original pack route over the summit of Winter Hill towards the village of Belmont, and then on to Blackburn.

In the early nineteenth century, there were several dwellings situated along the route over Winter Hill such as 'Five Houses', a group of terraced cottages, the Winter Hill Brick and Tile Works, and several small working coal pits, all owned by William Garbutt who resided at Five Houses. When excavations were being undertaken for the present television mast in 1959, old coal workings were discovered at a depth of some 50 feet. These were part of the Wildersmoor Colliery which was worked from the early nineteenth century until its eventual closure in 1961. At a distance of some 700 yards past the television mast, there is the site known locally as "Scotsman's Stump", where a simple memorial was erected to mark the spot where the victim of our case was discovered in 1838. It bears the following inscription:

> "In memory of George Henderson, native of Annan, Dumfrieshire, who was brutally murdered on Rivington Moor at noonday 9th November 1838, in the 20th year of his age."

'Scotsman's Stump' Pillar

Memorial Plaque on Pillar

Chapter One

Our account of the Winter Hill murder of November 1838, commences with the movements of one George Henderson, a twenty-year-old Scottish traveller, a native of Annan, Dumfriesshire. He was employed as a traveller by a Mr John Jardine, a draper with a business in Blackburn. Henderson moved around the neighbourhood stretching from Blackburn to the outskirts of Bolton, including surrounding small villages. He would spend his time selling goods, taking orders and collecting payment in return. It was his usual custom to make his way every other Friday back to Blackburn to report to his employer. This would take him on a regular route over Horwich Moor and Winter Hill to the village of Belmont.

He is known to have stayed overnight at the Old Cock Inn, in Manchester Road in the village of Blackrod on Thursday 8th November 1838. The following morning at the high vantage point of Blackrod, thick cloud could be seen smothering the nearby moors at Horwich and Winter Hill. It was in this general direction that the regular travellers' route to Blackburn ran, climbing up the moor and passing over the summit of Winter Hill, before descending to join the Bolton to Preston road near Belmont. About half a mile distance from the summit of Winter Hill and along the left-hand side of the road, stood a group of terraced cottages known locally as "Five Houses" or Garbutt's, after the owner of the cottages, brick and tile works and several local coal pits. Garbutt's own cottage also doubled as a beer-house which became a regular meeting place for both travellers and local inhabitants.

These travellers or 'packmen' were a common sight in the area during the nineteenth century, having migrated from Scotland to seek employment in the area. They often settled in small communities in towns of the north-west of England. One such area in Blackburn was known as "Nova Scotia" or "New Scotland". A fellow Scotsman, Benjamin Burrell, himself a traveller from Blackburn and friend of Henderson, had arranged to meet him on the Friday morning the 9th of November at about 11.00a.m. at Garbutt's beer-house. They were both due back in Blackburn on the Friday night, and had decided to have dinner together at the Black Dog Inn in Belmont, then travel back together.

Burrell had arrived at Garbutt's beer-house a little early on the Friday morning around 10.00a.m. and he waited until about 11.00a.m. for his companion to join him. Henderson not having arrived by then, Burrell left Garbutt's with a message that Henderson should join him later at Belmont for dinner. It is known that Henderson had left Blackrod on the Friday at around 8.00a.m., with his pack swung over his shoulder and a walking stick. His considerable delay in arriving at Garbutt's suggests that he may have made several calls along his route before eventually arriving at the beer-house around 12.00 noon. We are told that he did partake of a glass of ale which, according to Mr Garbutt, was a rare occurrence for the young Scotsman. Having received the message that Burrell had left some time earlier, he made his way up the road towards Winter Hill summit and on to Belmont.

At a point along the road not far from the summit and just before the road descends through a gateway in the boundary wall known as the "Stumps", the unfortunate traveller fell victim to an

horrific shooting from which injuries he subsequently
died. It was later estimated that the shooting must
have taken place between 12.15 and 12.30p.m. -
although there is some speculation as to the precise
time of the shooting. Henderson was still alive when a
young boy passing the spot heard moaning coming
from the drainage ditch on the right-hand side of the
road. He did not venture to the spot because of fear of
what he might find, but instead hurried to one of the
numerous coal-pits to raise the alarm. Returning
shortly in the company of one of the local colliers,
they both found Henderson who was lying on his
back in the ditch, having been shot through the head.
The time would have been around 12.45p.m. and with
the assistance of other local men who had by now
arrived at the scene, the victim was carried back down
the road to Garbutt's beer-house, where he died about
2.30p.m.

The body remained at Garbutt's for the post-
mortem examination until the following Wednesday,
when it was taken in solemn procession for burial in
Blackburn. According to Mr Jardine, Henderson's
employer, the deceased was a young man of goodly
appearance, pleasing in manner and of sober habits,
who was much respected by all those who knew him.
Such was the esteem in which he was held, that Mr
Jardine offered a reward of £100 for the apprehension
of the person or persons responsible for the shooting.

It later emerged from the extent of the injuries
suffered, that Henderson had been shot at very close
range, indicating a deliberate act rather than what was
at first suspected, a shooting accident. From the state
of certain items of the victim's clothing, robbery
appeared to have been a likely motive. The moors
around the area were well known for game, and as
such, they would attract not only those with

legitimate business there, but also poachers who would certainly have found the weather conditions on that day a distinct advantage for their clandestine work. Soon after the incident had been reported, a group of men who at the time had been observed on the moors with guns, were arrested on suspicion of being responsible for the shooting of Henderson. However, further enquiries revealed that they were, in fact, an organised shooting party from Smithills Hall and guests of the local landowner and magistrate, Peter Ainsworth.

The Blundell Arms, Horwich

Attention was focussed on a local collier, James Whittle, who lived with his parents in one of the cottages at "Five Houses" on the Winter Hill road. He was reported to have been seen on the moors that day with a gun. As a result, he was duly arrested on suspicion of the shooting and taken into custody. The Inquest into the death of Henderson was held on Tuesday 13th November 1838, at the Moorgate Inn, Horwich (now the Blundell Arms), and adjourned until Friday 16th November. After witnesses had given their evidence and further enquiries were completed, a verdict of 'Wilful Murder' was returned against James Whittle, and he was committed to Kirkdale Prison, Liverpool, to stand trial at the Lancashire Lent Assizes at Liverpool in 1839.

Press Reports of the Incident

"Horrible Murder at Belmont"

Bolton Chronicle,
Saturday November 10th, 1838

"Yesterday about one of the clock, one of the most dreadful and atrocious murders was committed in our neighbourhood which has now fallen our lot to report. It was with no common feeling of regret that we now take down to make public the gross act of great turpitude. Up to this time, the deed is wrapped in mystery. By the kindness of two medical gentlemen we have heard the particulars of the event and we are grieved to be compelled to make this public. All who know this country known that there are parts which are secluded and wild. Imagination pictures deeds of violence as we pass such tracks, and it was on one of these bare and barren spots that the murder was perpetrated. A poor itinerant Scotsman is the victim. With another of his countrymen, he was in the habit of travelling the county. The deceased was going by appointment to meet a friend at Five Houses near Two Lads, crossing from Horwich to Belmont. The non-appearance of the deceased induced the other Scotsman to go in search of him. The unhappy man discovered him by the roadside in a dying state, a shot having passed through his head, found its vent through the left eye. The face was terribly blackened. When found, he uttered, "I'm robbed, I'm killed".

His friend having to meet him, went back to the Black Dog at Belmont, where they ought to have dined, the dinner was ordered, but finding he did not come, he went in search of him. He states that while on his road, he met a tall man in shooting coat with a gun. He states that the stranger immediately lowered his gun and he saw him no more. He sought his friend and never heard of him until he heard of his death. No suspicion being attached to the man who gave evidence, he was allowed to go on his way and wept as he went to Blackburn. The body of the man presented a fearful spectacle. Mr Wright of Belmont was active in ascertaining as far as possible, the circumstances of the case immediately it was known. We are anxious as far as possible to give publicity to the murder that the circumstances being known, someone may perhaps be able to throw some light on the matter. The part of the country described is well-known. It was daylight when the murder was committed. The victim is dead and may be, we hope, identified, and we feel that no better way of getting information regarding this barbarous act, can be obtained than through the press, and hope the inhabitants of Blackburn will assist in the discovery and apprehending of the person who knew, and is likely to give some information regarding the individual in question."

Drainage Ditch on the Winter Hill Road.

"Horrid Murder at Horwich Moor near Bolton"

Blackburn Standard, Wednesday, November 14th, 1838

"We have of late observed with feelings of the utmost horror, the frequent recital in the public journals of the perpetration of barbarous and inhuman murders in the Sister Isle, but little did we think that we should be called upon to relate one of those dreadful instances of desperate depravity which reflects disgrace not merely on the age in which we live, but on human nature as occurring within the confines of our own country. It is our painful duty to give the particulars of a most horrid assassination which took place on Friday last at noon day on Horwich Moor about two miles from Belmont. On diverting from the Bolton Road to Belmont by the print works of Messrs Spencer and Winder, the traveller from Blackburn proceeds about half a mile up the New Preston Road to a gate 220 yards distant from the Wright's Arms.

On going through the gate, he proceeds along the base of a long chain of hills on his left, having a fine view to the right of Hill Top, the mansion of Thomas Wright Esq, and on the left a modern ruin called the Sheep Folds. On arriving at the top of Winter Hill, elevation 1,500 feet above sea level, we enter Horwich Moor the scene of the dreadful event. About half a mile from the nearest house by the side of the road, the victim of this deadly attack was shot in open day and thrown into the ditch. The bed of the ditch was covered with a small quantity of water. The deceased who was a traveller in the employ of Mr. John Jardine in this town, had travelled from

Blackrod early in the morning and was proceeding on his road homewards through the moor when his further progress was arrested by the deadly hand of the assassin."

Blackburn Standard, Saturday 17th November 1838

"Yesterday an Inquest was held before William Smalley Rutter, Gentleman, Coroner, at the Moorgate Inn, in the parish of Horwich, on the body of George Henderson who was found on Friday morning last, lying in a ditch in a wounded state. The Jury assembled precisely at eleven o'clock having viewed the body of the deceased previously which had laid at a beer-shop at Five Houses about two miles distant. The following were sworn onto the Jury:

Mr. Richard France, Foreman.
Mr. Titus Barlow.
Mr. John Pendlebury.
Mr. William Longworth.
Mr. John Hopwood.
Mr. Thomas Markland.
Mr. Hugh Grundy.
Mr. Richard Crankshaw.
Mr. Robert Barlow.
Mr. John Knowles.
Mr. Richard Booth.
Mr. Robert Orrell.
Mr. Joseph Winter.
Mr. James Spencer.
Mr. William Longworth.

Thomas Whowell stated that he resided at Holden's Farm on Smithills Moor with his grandfather Thomas Walsh. On the Friday morning he was going with his brother's dinner to the coal-pit on Winter Hill. He saw a Scotsman pass by carrying a bundle at the end of his stick. He passed him about

100 yards. As he was going straight along the road from Five Houses to the Winter Hill Tunnel, he heard a moan and looking up the road, he discovered several spots of blood. He was terrified and set off running immediately to the Tunnel to get some help. James Fletcher who was getting his dinner, came back with him to the spot where he heard the moaning. Moving on to the ditch he observed the Scotsman who he had seen passing that morning lying on his back in the water. There was blood then flowing from his head. Fletcher and he could not lift him and so he sent for further assistance. The blood in the road was about three yards from where the victim lay. There were no marks as if the body had been drawn across the road. From the place to the Tunnel was about 400 yards. The bundle and the stick were lying at the edge of his feet, He spoke only once when he and Fletcher got to him. He said, "Oh Jamie, Jamie, they have robbed me". From the time he heard the moaning to the time he got to the coal pit he saw no other person about the moor. It was terribly misty. He could see no more than a yard or so before him. Fletcher was the very first man who saw him after he got to the coal pit. He did not hear a gun going off. When he saw the Scotsman pass, he was perfectly sober. The breeches pockets of the deceased were turned out. There was not sufficient water in the ditch to cover the body. He could not tell who he meant when he said "Jamie". He heard no report of a gun on the moor at this time. When he got to the Tunnel, he found Fletcher's daughter there. There was no one else. The daughter had brought her father's dinner from Horwich.

James Fletcher stated that he lived at Horwich and was a banksman. The pit where the boy came from was the pit at which he was employed. It was distant from the Tunnel 400 to 500 yards. On Friday last he was opening a delph at the side of Winter Hill gate, a short distance from the Tunnel. His daughter had brought his dinner to the pit and, as it was rather wet, they went to the Tunnel. Continuing towards the 'Stumps', he heard the noise of a gun being fired. He said to his daughter that it was rather rare game for the poachers that day, for the keepers couldn't see them. From the delph to the Tunnel was about 160 yards, and from the Tunnel to the pit was about the same distance. When the boy came to the Tunnel, he had been there about ten minutes. The boy came running to the Cabin door. He said he had seen some blood and thought a man had been killed for he heard a moaning noise. He went back with him and discovered the deceased lying in a gutter by the side of the road. The body was in some water. He could not lift him out, so he sent his daughter to Garbutt's for assistance. He lifted the victim on the side of the bank, and he gave a deep sigh. Ho observed that he had a parcel to send off on Monday and then he said, "Damn them", after which he put his hand to his nose and in an attempt to blow it, the blood rushed out of the socket of the left eye, the other eye had obtruded itself from the socket more than two or three inches.

He had been shot and the mass of the shot had passed just under the right ear. Thomas Ratcliffe came and assisted him to get the deceased out of the ditch. When they got him out, they found the waistband of the breeches undone, except one button, and the right-hand breeches pocket was turned out. He laid the body on the ground and rested the head on his knee until a chair was brought. They then carried him down to his master's, where the body now lies. He remained with him until he died which was about half-past two the same afternoon. The brains came

through the eye which was blown out. The cheek and
under the ear were stained with powder marks, and
the roots of the ear or eye were projecting out. The
wound at the ear seemed as if it had been made by the
muzzle of a gun put against it. The brains were lying
scattered about the road. There was no damage done
to any other part of his dress. After he heard the
report of the gun, he saw no person about. There had
been a tramp in the Cabin in the morning. The report
of the gun was not distant, and it came from the
direction in which the boy ran from. It was the report
of a gun, not a pistol, such a fire as might come from
a sportsman. He had never seen anyone with a gun
that morning, and that was the only report he had
heard that day. It was not such a day as a sportsman
would select for shooting because it was so misty.

James Ratcliffe stated that he lived at Horwich
and was one of Mr Garbutt's banksmen. The first that
he heard of this was from Fletcher's daughter who
came running down the road to the coal pit. She told
him that her father had sent her for him to help get a
man out of the ditch. He went and assisted him. His
master and Whittle's father came up, and Mr Garbutt
sent Whittle's father for the doctor and a constable.
We then carried the deceased down to Five Houses,
and he saw the wound on the Scotsman's ear which
was blackened with powder. He did not hear the
report of any gun. He was working at the pit about
600 or 700 yards from the spot where the deceased
lay. When the boy Whowell came he was in the
Cabin eating his dinner. He had not seen anyone with
a gun that day. He had seen the first Scotsman
passing an hour before in the direction of Belmont.
He saw him afterwards that day, when he was sent for
from Belmont by Mr Garbutt. He said to him on
hearing the particulars of the murder, "It might have

been me". The coal pit where he worked is near the road. He did not know the Scotsman.

Mary Entwistle was the daughter of James Fletcher and was at the Tunnel with her father when the boy came in. She lived in Horwich and took her father's dinner to the stone pit on Friday. She went the road the Scotsman did. It was about 12.30p.m. when she arrived. She knew the boy Whowell, but she had not seen him before he came to the Tunnel. She heard the gun fired but saw no other person about. After the boy came, they went with him to where the deceased lay. She went to the pit to Ratcliffe for assistance and afterwards to Garbutt's for the same reason. Mr. Garbutt was at home and accompanied her and John Whittle (the prisoner's father) back to where the body was lying. She then went home. At about 8.30a.m. that morning she saw Whittle with a gun shooting near her house. She thought he had the same clothes on then as he had now. She was sure that it was him for she knew him well. She never saw anyone with a gun besides him that day. He was firing upon the moor at some moor game, but he missed them. Her house is in the hollow near to Five Houses. She did not go into Garbutt's house to give the alarm but shouted out and told him that a man was lying in a ditch. Both Mr Garbutt and his wife came out. Whittle's house is a door or two from Garbutt's and the prisoner lives with his father and mother there. She lives about 200 yards away in what they called Quaker John's House. She did not see the prisoner again until 5.00p.m. when he was standing by Garbutt's.

William Garbutt stated that he knew the deceased by sight, in consequence of his regularly passing his home, but he never frequented his home during his travels. About noon on Friday last, he came in for the last time. He was alone when he came in, and he called for a glass of ale and drank it off twice. When he came in, the two carters were already in the house. This was about 20 minutes before the girl came in to give the alarm. He had seen Whittle before that day in the forenoon. At daylight he heard someone firing on the moor. The prisoner's father was that morning getting in some potatoes for him. He said, '...there is a great deal of shooting going on this morning'. He replied '...yes, I have seen some smoke twice'. While talking to his father, he saw some person which he believed was the prisoner, come through the hedge bottom with a gun in his hand, just before he had heard three reports of a gun. This was about 9 or 10.00a.m. He was never seen at his home after the dead body was brought in, but his wife told him that she had seen the prisoner look into the window on the Friday morning whilst the deceased Scotsman was still inside. "Robert Makin, Constable of Halliwell stated that he informed the prisoner of the charge on which he was being arrested. He had asked, 'Have you seen the Scotsman?' Whittle had replied 'Yes, I have seen him and spoken to him'. The constable then asked him how he knew it was the man. He replied, 'From the description that had been given afterwards'. He then asked him what kind of person he was and what dress he wore. The prisoner replied that he could not tell. He afterwards said in the lockup, on being asked by the constable what had killed the deceased, that it was not a bullet but slugs. He then stated that he had been on the moors that morning but with no gun on him.

An adjourned Inquest was held on Friday 16th November 1838. Thomas Rutterworth, residing at Blackrod, stated that he knew the deceased. He was in the same way of business as the deceased. He was in business on his own account and had seen Henderson on the Thursday night and had stayed with him at the Cock Inn at Blackrod. He saw him start on his road homeward at 8.00a.m. He had no opportunity of knowing what money he had about him. He heard him call for some port wine at the Inn which he paid for in silver. The Coroner addressed the prisoner, "Whittle, the evidence is now closed. Now is the time for you to say anything in your defence or to call any witness to prove where you were at the time when this horrid transaction took place". Whittle protested his innocence and said that he hadn't anything further to say than that he was at home at the time when the alarm was given, and also at Five Houses at 12.00 noon, adding that his father could prove this. A proclamation for witnesses for the defence was announced, but not a single person offered to come forward. The prisoner was about 22 years of age, six feet tall, possessing a dark, morose, unpleasant countenance, but strong and athletic form. He has of late been a lawless, dissolute and reckless character, known for poaching. His habits of indolence had been latterly more confirmed, having formed an illicit connection with a young woman in the area to whom it is said, he was to have been married in the week previous to the murder."

The Manchester Times,
Saturday 17th November 1838

"Several witnesses were examined who proved the prisoner was at Five Houses on the day in question at 12.00 noon, and that at the time the deceased passed Five Houses, the prisoner was seen to leave his father's house and go in the direction of where the deceased's body was found afterwards. The prisoner was committed to Kirkdale for trial at the Liverpool Assizes."

Wheeler's Manchester Chronicle, Saturday 17th November 1838

"George Henderson was shot through the head by some villain and his pockets rifled after which the body was thrown into a ditch by the road side. He (the accused) had a single barrelled gun which was a percussion piece. The Coroner asked the prisoner if he had any witnesses to prove where he was at the time of the murder. The prisoner's father John Whittle appeared very much agitated and stated that his son was at home when the murder was committed."

Horwich, its History, Legends and Church, Thomas Hampson, 1883

"About 10.00a.m. in the morning, Mr Benjamin Burrell, the friend referred to, arrived at Five Houses and went into the beer-shop kept by Mr. W. Garbutt, where he waited for half an hour. We have to add that Roger Horrocks, who was found in a turf-cess with a gun at his side, was at one time supposed to be the guilty party, but closer evidence fixed upon a man names James Whittle, the former was liberated, and the latter arrested. On Tuesday, November 13th, the Inquest was held and in consequence of the reports that were current on Friday and Saturday, Thomas Wright Esquire and Peter Ainsworth had thought it right to direct the arrest of a collier named James Whittle who was in the employ of the latter. William Garbutt, beer-seller and master collier, said he lived at Five Houses, Horwich. There are no other houses on the road but those between Horwich and Belmont. A girl informed him in the forenoon of that day. He recollected seeing him fire a gun at the bottom of his garden on Friday morning. He saw Whittle pass by his house while the Scotsman was inside. There was no other company. Many people came in to see the body, but he did not see Whittle amongst them. Burrell, the surviving Scotsman, said he was going to Belmont and saw a man near the place where Henderson was found, above the hill, and he had a gun. A verdict of Wilful Murder was returned against Whittle. The trial took place at Liverpool Crown Court on Tuesday, April 2nd, 1839."

The Manchester Courier, Saturday November 17th, 1838

"Adjourned Inquest - Yesterday morning at 10.00a.m. the adjourned Inquest was held. Daniel Cook, Constable of Sharples, was called in. He said that he had been sent for by Mr Wright to apprehend at the coal-pit, Whittle who worked there. The Constable of Halliwell took him into custody. The prisoner said he had no gun with him on Friday afternoon, and that he was out with Mr. Matthew Lambert. He said that he had shot a bird that day but couldn't remember what kind. Henderson had made an appointment with another Scotsman, Benjamin Burrell, to meet on the road over the moor and dine at Belmont. Burrell arrived at Five Houses about 10.00a.m. and he waited at Mr. Garbutt's beer-house. He waited about one and a half hours, and then left a message that he would meet Henderson at dinner in Belmont. At approximately 12 noon, the deceased arrived at Garbutt's and was told that Burrell had gone on, so he hastened on. At about 12.15p.m. the body was found, and there was a coal-pit about 300 yards from the spot. One of the banksmen took Henderson by the hand and said, "I think you are hurt, sir". The deceased replied, "I am robbed, Jamie, and I should have sent a parcel off on Monday". He was immediately removed to Garbutt's who, on hearing the news, got all the workpeople out of the pits, and the moors were scoured in all directions. From various circumstances which came to light, it was deemed necessary to apprehend James Whittle, a young man of 22, who resides next door to Garbutt's and is employed as a collier at Mr. Ainsworth's pit in Halliwell.

Garbutt immediately sent men on horseback to Belmont for Mr. Burrell. On his return, he stated that when he arrived near the spot, a tall white looking young man dressed in blue clothes with a gun in his hand asked him, "Is there any game about here?" Burrell replied, "I believe there is". Whittle then said, "If you go with me a bit, you shall have the first that I kill". Burrell declined the offer saying that he had business to attend to. After walking a few yards, he turned to see the man with the gun levelled as if to shoot him. He pretended to have been aiming at birds. Burrell proceeded but kept an eye on the man as he went. When this was related, suspicion fell immediately on Whittle who was exactly the sort of person described in both dress and appearance. Whittle was also seen opposite Mr. Garbutt's house without a gun at the time the alarm was given. He made off without rendering any assistance and did not return until night. He also led a dissolute life of late. Mr Jardine, the deceased's employer, had met Henderson on Tuesday night at Preston, and received all the money he had collected upon his journey. Mr Jardine conjectures that he could not have had more than £15 about him at the time of the murder. According to a witness, Thomas Whowell, Henderson passed him about 12.30p.m. carrying a bundle on the end of a stick. He heard moaning about half a mile from the pit, and a further 10 yards, he saw blood on the road.

George Wolstenholme, Surgeon of Little Bolton, examined the head of the deceased. There was a wound in the right temple, and the frontal bone was fractured from one temple to the other. The left eye was carried away completely. He took off the front part of the skull and ascertained that the posterior part of the eyeball was carried away, as well as the bone which forms the roof of the orbit, and which supports the anterior lobes of the brain. Most of that portion of bone was carried away. He found in the brain, six pieces of lead which are either shot or slugs. He believed that the principal part of the shot escaped through the left eye. Every part of the brain was perfectly healthy except part of the anterior lobes which were lacerated. This injury had caused death. He thought that the person who shot must have had a gun or pistol very near, as the shot was not scattered, and the wound was about one inch in diameter."

Bolton Chronicle,
Saturday 24th November 1838

"About 12.00 noon on Wednesday 14th
November, the funeral procession started from Five
Houses at which time there were not about a dozen
spectators. The coffin which contained the body, was
of good substantial oak, the inscription on the plate
merely denoting the name and age of the deceased.
The corpse was placed in the hearse by six of Mr
Wright's servants who were in attendance at Five
Houses by his direction. Also attended Whittle's
father who witnessed the spectacle with emotions of
deepest sorrow. The hearse was followed by a
carriage containing the employer and three other
friends of the deceased.

Mr. W. Jardine, Mr. J. Jardine, Mr. P. Johnson
and Mr. G. Brown rode in the procession. The
cavalcade passed the spot where the murder was
perpetrated and continued to course over Winter Hill
to the New Preston Road whence diverging to the left,
it proceeded to Belmont and then fell into Bolton
Road. It reached the village of Over Darwen about
3.30p.m. The streets were lined with spectators from
the Bowling Green Inn at Livesey Fold. On arriving
at the Crown Inn at Nova Scotia, the cortege was met
by Rev. Francis Skinner, Minister to the Scottish
Church, and twenty-five of his countrymen attended.
The procession moved towards Blackburn, and
passed through Darwen Street, Church Street and
Salford Street, reaching the Presbyterian Church in
Mount Street at 5.00p.m. The chapel was crowded to
excess with not less than 1,000 present. The following
Sunday afternoon, the Rev. Skinner in his funeral
discourse, used the text, "In the day of adversity,
consider".

Chapter Two

The Trial

R v WHITTLE

Lancashire Lent Assizes - Liverpool Crown Court

Tuesday 2nd April 1829

Before

Lord Justice Baron Parke

James Whittle aged 22 was arraigned on a Charge of having wilfully murdered one George Henderson on Friday 9th November 1838 on Horwich Moor by the discharging at him of a loaded gun.

PLEADED NOT GUILTY.

Counsel for the Prosecution:

Messrs Dundas, Peel and Cross.

Instructing Attorney: Mr. Holden of Bolton.

Counsel for the Defence:

Mr. Sergeant Wilkins.

Instructing Attorney: Mr. Taylor of Bolton.

Plan of the Area of the Killing – Jonathan Hardman, Surveyor, Bolton 1838.

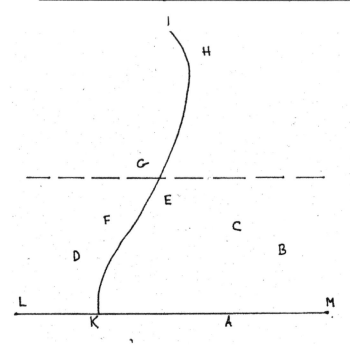

A = Wright's Arms, Belmont.
B = Belmont Print Works.
C = 'Hill Top', Belmont.
D = Ruins of Sheep Folds.
E = The 'Cabin' at the Winter Hill Tunnel.
F = The place where Burrell met the man with the gun.
G.= The spot where Henderson's body was found.
H = Five Houses and Garbutt's Beer-house.
I - K = The Winter Hill Road.
L - M = The Bolton to Preston Road.

Hardman's Plan of the Area of the Shooting - 1838.

Witness Statements

Jonathan Hardman

Jonathan Hardman, a surveyor from Bolton, produced a plan of the area of the killing, which showed Five Houses as a group of cottages on Winter Hill. They were known locally as 'Garbutt's' after the owner William Garbutt, whose cottage was used as a beer-house for the use of miners, packmen and travellers. He indicated that the distance from Garbutt's to the spot where Henderson's body was discovered was 972 yards. Nearby was the entrance to one of the coal mines called the Tunnel. The distance from the spot to the Stumps which was a boundary wall five feet in height, was 212 yards. The distance from the Stumps to the Tunnel was 137 yards. The Moorgate Inn at Horwich was approximately 2 miles distance from Garbutt's. There was no footpath between Horwich Moorgate and Five Houses, so people crossed over the moor. On the moor were numerous ditches cut for drainage. Lying between the spot where Henderson's body was found, and the Winter Hill road was a deep ditch approximately 3 feet wide, which was extended on the right side of the road from Five Houses to the Stumps.

Thomas Whowell

Thomas Whowell, a boy of 14, worked for Thomas Walsh of Horwich, and was riding on the morning of the 9th November near to Adam Hill which was about half a mile from Garbutt's. He was on his way to see his brother who worked in one of the mines on Winter Hill. Whilst he was on Adam Hill, he heard the midday bell ring from Ridgeway's

Works in Horwich. When he arrived at Garbutt's, he
saw the Scotsman come out and go up the road.
Thomas's horse was making heavy going up the hill,
so he swore at it. When he came to the pit, he stopped
to take his brother's dinner. The Scotsman was
walking with a stick and bundle on his back and came
up to him and reproved him for swearing. It was
custom to call any packman Scotsman, because many
travelling packmen originated from Scotland. The pit
was approximately 400 yards from Garbutt's.
He stopped with his brother for about ten minutes and
then began his journey down the road. After going
about 300 yards from the pit, he heard a moaning
noise coming from the ditch on the side of the road. A
bit further on, he noticed blood on the ground. He was
afraid and did not look into the ditch but went
forward to the Tunnel where he saw James Fletcher
together with his daughter Mary Entwistle. He told
them what he had heard, and they went with him to
the place where they found the Scotsman lying in the
ditch. It was the same man he had seen going up the
road. Fletcher tried to lift him - but he could not.
Thomas went for assistance and met Garbutt and John
Whittle (the prisoner's father) coming up the road. He
had known the prisoner for about two years, and he
was in the habit of shooting. The day was very misty,
and he could not see far before him. He heard the
moaning about 12.30 to 12.45p.m. The deceased
appeared to be in great agony and struggled much
with his hands. He did not notice any footmarks near
the place where he lay. He did not see a gun or a
pistol near the spot - or see the body when he passed
it first time. The bundle was lying beside the deceased
in the ditch and did not appear to have been opened.
He did not observe that the pockets were turned out.

James Fletcher

James Fletcher, a bankman at the coal pit near to Five Houses, stated that on the 9th November, he was working in a stone delph on Horwich Moor near the Tunnel. About 12.30p.m. his daughter came with his dinner and he went with her to the Cabin to eat it. This was used by quarry workers and miners to eat their food. When near to the Stumps, he heard the report of a gun from the right of Five Houses. Whilst getting his dinner in the Cabin, Thomas Whowell came in, and in consequence of what he had stated, he went with him to the place where the body lay. Whowell pointed out the spot and when he went back to it, he discovered the deceased lying on his back. One of the eyes was entirely blown out.

When Thomas Ratcliffe (another banksman) came up, they lifted the body out of the ditch. When they looked, they saw that the right-hand pocket hung over the trousers on the outside, and they were torn down from the pocket. He did not observe that the left pocket was turned out in the same way. They carried the deceased to Mr. Garbutt's as soon as possible, where he died at about 2.30p.m. His right ear was much discoloured and black with powder. They were assisted by William Garbutt, James Heaton, James Bamford and a man named Lomax. He was placed on a table; the body being washed, and the eye replaced in its socket. He did not see any firearms near the site, but many blood stains on the ground close to it. In the left waistcoat pocket, Fletcher and his friends found one shilling and eleven pence. In Fletcher's opinion, the trousers appeared to have been unbuttoned by force. When asked if it would have been possible for a person firing the fatal shot to have reached the Cabin without being seen on the road, Fletcher said it was impossible. The person firing the shot would have to cross the moor and get to the Cabin without Fletcher seeing him. Fletcher had about 130 yards to go after hearing the shot, whereas the man would have to go about 300 yards. On his return to the Cabin, there was a man about fifty years of age asleep there. He was a stranger to the neighbourhood, and he thought that he was a 'navvy'. He had a stick and a bundle attached to it. He was dressed in fustian trousers and had a blue waistcoat, and on awakening he left the Cabin.

Thomas Ratcliffe

Thomas Ratcliffe had been working in the coal pit next to Five Houses. Mary Entwistle had come to him and after hearing the story, he went to the site where the victim lay. The ditch was about half a yard deep and of a similar width. He heard the gun fired below Five Houses on the other side of the pit about 10.00a.m. He had not heard a shot about 12.00 noon because the wind was blowing towards the Stumps. He had never known Whittle to do any harm to anyone and described him as good-tempered and well-behaved.

Site of the Winter Hill Tunnel

William Stott

William Stott was aged 13 years and was examined by Mr. James Cross, partner in the firm of Cross and Kay, Attorneys, Bolton. He worked in the Tunnel where he had been on the day in question. He had seen Whittle inside the Cabin at about 11.00a.m. in the morning. When he had seen Whittle, he had asked him the time and had been told 11.00a.m. Whittle had been dressed in the clothes he was now wearing. With Whittle in the Cabin had been William Simms and an old tramp, but he could not remember how Simms was dressed. Asked why, he replied that Whittle had been closer to him and it was dark in the Cabin. He went to the Tunnel and was there about ten minutes, and when he next looked in the Cabin, Simms had gone but Whittle was still inside with the tramp. He then made a rather strange statement saying that he had been approached privately and told to keep to the same story. He had also been informed that there was a £100 reward to be had and had been instructed to say what colour Whittle's clothes were. On reflection, he was sure Simm's jacket had been dark, and he had gone into the Cabin to shelter from the rain.

William Fletcher

William Fletcher was the son of James Fletcher and had been working at Garbutt's on the day in question, in place of James Heaton. He left work about 11.00a.m. and on his way home he had seen Whittle in an old road near to a 'turf-cess' which was between the pit and Garbutt's house. He had a gun in his hand. Whittle asked if he had a 'play-day' (a day off) - and he replied he had from that time for the rest of the day. They then walked together until they were about three fields away from his home. It was about 11.45a.m. when he arrived home. Whittle had left him between Five Houses and the pit.

Sarah Lomax

Sarah Lomax lived at Five Houses between Whittle's and Garbutt's, and she was at home when the killing took place. Before she had heard the news of the killing, she had seen Whittle coming from the direction of the spot where the body was found. This would be about 12.00 noon. Whittle was standing in the cart road near the house.

Anne Garbutt

Anne Garbutt lived next door to Sarah Lomax and was also at home on the 9th November. From her window she had seen Whittle go past at about 12.00 noon and Henderson was still in her house.

Immediately Whittle passed, Henderson went out. Twenty minutes later, she saw Whittle again through her window, this time he was coming from the direction of Horwich a little before the murder. The first time he was going towards Belmont and the second time he was coming from his own door and was not wearing a hat. She definitely saw Whittle pass her window around 12.10p.m. A stranger on a grey pony called at about 2.30p.m.

William Heaton

William Heaton was a carrier for Garbutt and between 10.00 and 11.00a.m. on the 9th November, he was going up Winter Hill from the Belmont side with a horse and cart. At the bottom of the hill he met William Simms going in the direction of Belmont. Late he met Burrell going in the same direction. He stopped to load his cart at the delph where James Fletcher was working. He then went on to Garbutt's reaching it about 12.00 noon, where he found Bamford inside. He had been in about twenty minutes when Whittle came in and asked about a horse being ill. Two or three minutes later, Mary Entwistle came down the road shouting, and by then, Whittle was on his way out.

Benjamin Burrell

Benjamin Burrell stated that in the month of November, he was living in Blackburn, and was in the service of a Mr. John Foster as his traveller. He knew George Henderson who, last November was also in the service of Mr. John Jardine of Blackburn. He was about twenty years of age and was a fellow Scotsman. It was their practice to go certain routes to sell goods, take orders and collect money, and this was one of the duties of the deceased. Both their rounds took them over Horwich Moor to Belmont. They went across the moor every other Friday, and the 9th November was one such day. When they got home in Blackburn, they accounted for the fortnight's proceeds. He knew Garbutt's beer-house and on the 9th November, they appointed to meet there a little after 11.00a.m. He went to Garbutt's according to his arrangement and reached there about 10.00a.m. He remained there till about 11.00a.m. and since Henderson had not arrived, he left word that he had gone on to Belmont. When he left Garbutt's house, he went in the direction of a place called the 'Stumps', and he had seen the place where the body was found and had passed it alone on the 9th November. As he was going up the hill, one of the colliers called to him, 'Are you going up?' Near to the place where the body was found, he saw a man about 50 yards off, and he had a gun in his hand.

He came towards him as he went on and came off the moor onto the road behind him. There was a ditch between the road and the moor. When in the road, the man would have been about 10 to 12 yards away. He asked him if he had seen two men as he expected two to come off the moor. He was told that none had been seen. When he spoke, Burrell was near enough to see that he was a tall man dressed in dark clothes. The gun he had with him was a single-barrelled one. Burrell walked up the hill and the man walked behind him. After proceeding a few yards, he happened to look behind him and saw the man pointing the gun towards him about 10 yards off. When he turned around, the man asked him if he saw some birds but there were no birds in the direction in which the gun was pointed. The man came nearer, and Burrell asked him if he could shoot birds flying.

He said he could and that if he would go with him on the moor, he would give him or kill him a bird and show him a good path to Belmont. Burrell told him that he was going to Belmont because the man had enquired. After the conversations which took place as they were walking, he told Burrell that the path was against the wall and through the 'Stumps' and turn to the right. He went through the 'Stumps' and the man came close to him. He observed his clothes - his trousers were blue and very much worn about the knees, a patch was upon one of them and they were very short. He had a blue coat and a dark waistcoat. He wore his hat very much over the eyes. He had the opportunity of noticing his gun, which had a single barrel and a percussion cap. He couldn't swear that the man he saw was the prisoner, but he had the same general appearance, was wearing the same kind of clothes, and was about the same height. He heard Whittle speak at the Inquest, and the voice was very similar to that of the man on the moor. Not seeing the appearance of a footpath, Burrell told the man that he had business to attend to and turned back. He did not observe the man following him. He then went down the road to Belmont and met two carters with three carts and three horses. Their names were Heaton and Bamford. They were about 200 yards from the Belmont side of the Tunnel. He reached Belmont just before noon, and was sent for to Garbutt's, and reached there about 2.00p.m. He saw the deceased there who died about two minutes later.

Joseph Halliwell

Joseph Halliwell, when examined by Mr.
Dundas, stated that he was a corn-dealer carrying on a
business in Skipton. In November last, he was in the
service of Mr. Gerrard, another cattle-dealer from
Bolton. On the 9th November, he had directions to call
for a heifer at Walsh's Farm. He called at the place
where he worked and by his directions went to the
farm on Smithills Moor called Gilligant's. He saw
Mrs Hood there and arrived at the farm at 12.25p.m.
by her clock. He was not able to get the heifer and
remained at the farm for no more than ten minutes. It
was very foggy at the time. He was on his way to
Belmont, and asked Mrs Hood to direct him. She told
him that the road went to a place known as Holden's
Farm. The road by which he went led towards a brow,
and turning off to the right, this brought him onto
Smithills Moor. When he got some distance, he heard
the report of a gun. By then, he had lost his directions
and insisted that he was sober and had only three
glasses of ale on that day. He went in the direction of
the sound of the shooting thinking some gentleman
might be shooting and would tell him the road to
Belmont. He met the prisoner within a quarter of an
hour. When he first saw him, he was about 30 yards
off and it was very foggy indeed. The prisoner was
running towards him and had a gun in his right hand.
He got within a few yards of him when he spoke to
him and asked directions but got no answer. He was
dressed in a blue surcoat, blue trousers and a blue
waistcoat with a yellow spot. He thought it was the
same waistcoat he had on now. He was running in the
direction away from the sound which he had heard.
After going about 320 yards from the spot where he
met the prisoner, he came to a road. There was a ditch

between him and the road. He saw a man lying in the ditch, the right-hand pocket of his trousers was torn down. He got off his horse to look at him and saw blood on his cheek which turned him very sick. He attempted to get off the moor and onto the road. He was riding a grey pony but could not get it over the ditch. He tried two or three times in different places and went down the ditch 40 yards. He then remounted and then tried to go back again, but he could not tell in which direction he was going. When the mist cleared away, he found himself close to Holden's Farm where he had originally started off. He knew Garbutt's and got there between 2 and 3.00p.m. and had a glass of ale on his horse. He did not know at the time, that the body of the deceased was lying in the beer-house. He said nothing about the body in the ditch as he did not know anybody in that part and was apprehensive. He had on him £304.16s. 6d. of his own money. In going along the road to Garbutt's, he saw a man and his wife about twenty yards from the place where the body was found.

Cross-Examination of Halliwell by Mr Wilkins (Defence Counsel)

Halliwell had stated that he had been a cattle-dealer ever since last Christmas, buying and selling for both himself and other people. He had bought off a man near Giggleswick in Yorkshire perhaps half a dozen times, but he did not know his name particularly. He couldn't say how many times he had bought from John Wilson, a butcher and cattle-dealer from Colne. He had bought calving cows off him since last Christmas but couldn't say how many, or how much he paid or how often. He had received £304 by his own labour and had brought from home that day. He lived with his mother and was a drover. She was a widow and lived in a cottage and subsisted on what he gave her. His father had also been a drover but left no property. When he first started out as a drover, he earned a shilling a day and his expenses. He was then only 14 years of age. He had from Mr. Gerrard 24 shillings a week when he was in his service, amounting to £62.10s a year, and he had calculated this amount before coming to court, knowing that he might be asked such a question. The money was left at his mother's cottage in Yorkshire until the Monday week before he started. She gave it to him at that time, and he had shown it to no one else. It was in notes. The rent of her small cottage was £3 a year.

He did not know at what time he got up that morning. He swapped a cow with a Mr Webster of Footed Brook that very morning. He let him have a beast of his that he got from him a week before - and another one. They had a glass of ale over their swap. They went back to Mr. Gerrard's, then to a beer-house and had only one glass of ale. He paid for another man's ale while there too. They had a six-weeks reckoning and settled their accounts at Mr. Gerrard's. He paid him seven shillings and sixpence or fifteen shillings and sixpence - he couldn't say exactly which. He left Gerrard's at 10.00a.m. and the horse he rode was Mr. Gerrard's. The first place he stopped at after passing St. George's Church in Little Bolton was Mr. Ainsworth's pits. Though he stopped at the first pit, he did not see John Entwistle eating his dinner. He saw another man at the first pit, but he did not get off his horse. He would swear that he did not ask the way to the Green's Arms. The man directed him to Ainsworth's pits, and he met up with John Walsh there. He asked him to drive his heifer for him – it was a heifer which his master had bought from Walsh's master. He did not ask the way to Gilligant's Farm. He asked him if he could cross two fields, but he said he could not, although he went across them anyway. It was between 11.00 and 12.00 noon when he got to the pit. He met Walsh's wife within 20 yards of the pit with his dinner.

He did not know Richard Nuttall. He offered a man 1s. 6d to help him with the heifer over the moor. He may have called him Dick. At this time, he had not yet seen the dead man. When he got to Gilligant's, he saw a clock and asked who had made it. He noticed it was not 1.25p.m. by that clock. He was not drunk and did not fall off his horse. He did not remember losing his whip and he did not tell Grace Whowell that he was so drunk he could not drive the heifer. He did not know the country there at all, nor did he know Garbutt's House or Quaker John's. It was a little after 2.00p.m. when he arrived at Five Houses and it was about two hours since he had last seen the body. He could not swear to the dress of the wounded man. His pack was laid upon the opposite side of the road in the ditch. He did not jump over the ditch himself. He asked his road to the Wright's Arms and he did not know whether he had told anyone what he had seen. He got to Proctor's at half-past three. John Proctor was landlord of the Duckworth Arms at Over Darwen on the main turnpike road between Bolton and Blackburn. He told him that he believed it was a Scotsman shot that day. He supposed it was a Scotsman from his pack. He told Mr. Proctor that he had seen the body and a person running from that direction with a gun on Horwich Moor. An Irishman and his wife whom he overtook on the road, told him a man had been murdered. He was fetched from Yorkshire to give evidence a week afterwards.

He never heard of the £100 reward being offered. He left Gerrard's service the Monday after Christmas Day, and on his solemn oath would swear he never heard of the reward being offered. The Constables of Blackburn and Bolton together with others, told him to look at the prisoner in the lock-up. He told them he would not swear to him by candlelight. The day afterwards, he saw him at Horwich Moorgate Inn at the Inquest, and then swore to him. He described the prisoner to the constable the Thursday night after the murder before he had seen him in the lock-up. What he said was written down by Mr. Perris, Constable of Blackburn. He mentioned everything as he had given it this day. On the evening, he was fetched from Westhoughton by Thomas Ellis, a drover who'd come from Yorkshire to see him.

Re-Examination by Mr. Dundas
(Counsel for the Prosecution)

Mr. Proctor lives at Over Darwen and it was 3.30p.m. when he told him what he had seen. He showed him a piece of the man's skull which the Irishman, gave him, and which he said he had picked up on the opposite side of the road to where the man was lying. He couldn't say whether he gave an account of it to the people he saw at the Wright's Arms at Belmont. He knew the man very well when he saw him at the Inquest and had no doubt that he was the same he had met on the moor with a gun.

William Garbutt

He stated that he kept a beer-house at Five Houses, knew Henderson quite well and was at home on the Friday. The other Scotsman called every other Friday on business between Horwich and Blackburn, and often changed silver and sovereigns for notes. Henderson was not a regular caller at the beer-house. At the time Mary Entwistle came with the news, Whittle was standing close to his right side, but he had no gun with him, and this would be about 1.00p.m. He had seen Whittle that morning about 8.00a.m. with a gun. He had also seen a person of about his height and dress similarly fire a gun on three separate occasions. About 10.00a.m. he again saw Whittle, and then finally about 1.00p.m. leaving his house. He did not see him again that day. Many people came to see the body, but he did not see Whittle amongst them. The early part of the morning had been clear, but it became foggy about noon. It cleared in the afternoon, so that men could be seen on the moors at a considerable distance. These proved to be a shooting party. Burrell had exchanged some money when he called at the beer-house, but not Henderson.

Mrs. Lambert

She lived at the Moorgate Inn, Horwich, and stated that she had been at home on the 9th November and had seen Whittle about 1.30p.m. She had spoken to him and asked about her husband's gun, one which had been lost sometime before. Whittle had told her that he knew nothing at all about it. He was still at the Moorgate at 3.00p.m. A servant came in and said that there had been a man shot on the moor - a Scotsman. Whittle then remarked that many of them went that way on Friday on their way home. He then stated that two or three of them made appointments to meet there on Friday and go home together. He then said that he had brought back the gun he had borrowed and would never have another one in his house while he lived. She said that Whittle had left the house about 4.00p.m. She also stated that she heard of Mr. Orrell, the steward of Mr. Wright's estate who had called at Whittle's house to complain to his father about Whittle poaching on the moor. Whittle stated that he had not shot fowl as he came through Brownlow's Close, which lay between Five Houses and the Moorgate Inn.

Mr. Matthew Lambert

He was the landlord of the Horwich Moorgate Inn, and he agreed that on Thursday 8th November he had lent the prisoner a single barrel fowling piece with a percussion cap. He made an appointment to meet him on the Friday in Brownlow's Close, about 1½ miles from the Moorgate. Whittle had stayed at the inn until about 4.00p.m. on the Friday. Before leaving the inn, Lambert asked Whittle about the shooting of the packman, and queried as to whether it was accidental or a wilful act? Whittle had replied that he did not know any details about it, but if it had been done deliberately then whoever had fired the shot, deserved to suffer for it. He stated that he thought it was not quite 1.30p.m. when Whittle arrived at the Moorgate. The foreman of the Jury asked what size of shot was in the shot bag, and Lambert stated that it was No 2 shot, and had been taken away in the shot bag by John Whittle, the Chief Constable of Wigan. The gun which had not been loaded when it was brought back, was handed over to Mr. Peter Heron who was a gun expert. The charge in the gun was not withdrawn. The weapon had been handed over at the Coroner's request to Constable Burrows. On the Friday, Whittle came to the Moorgate and brought a pair of grouse still warm. He reared the gun against the wall of the brew-house and went inside. They both left at 4.00p.m. and went in search of a hare up to the north of Brownlow's Close. He walked back with Whittle for about 600-700 yards, and then came back home again. Before leaving, Whittle explained he had brought the gun back and everything belonging to it.

Mary Cross

Stated that she was employed by Mr. Lambert at the Moorgate Inn and had seen Whittle on the Friday between 10.00 and 10.30a.m. in the back yard. There is a meadow behind the inn, and she saw Whittle come across this with a gun in his hand. They had heard about the murder at about 3.30p.m. and the prisoner had left the Moorgate at about 4.00p.m.

When Whittle had arrived, he had some birds with him which were still warm and obviously recently shot. She was not quite sure whether it was near to 12.30 or 1.00p.m. when the prisoner arrived at the Moorgate, but it was somewhere about that time.

Mary Entwistle

Mary was James Fletcher's daughter who had accompanied her father from the Tunnel to the stone delph and heard the report of a gun at some time around 12.30p.m. She went for help to Garbutt's. She knew James Whittle and had seen him on the Friday morning about 8.30a.m. between Five Houses and Entwistle Lane. He had a gun with him and was wearing a long blue coat, blue trousers and a blue waistcoat. The time from hearing the gun report and Whowell coming to inform her father about the incident was about thirty minutes. She had not seen Whittle on her way and had not seen him fire that morning.

George Wolstenholme

He was a surgeon practising in Higher Bridge Street, Little Bolton, and stated that he had performed a post-mortem examination on George Henderson on Monday 12th November. There was a gunshot wound on the right temple as a bullet or slug had passed through, carrying away the right eye. In the brain, he had found six pieces of shot and in his opinion, the victim had died as a result of this injury. The lead shot weighed 18 drams and was No 3 shot. He had weighed the shot with others bought from Samuel Cartwright, Ironmonger of 154, Deansgate, Bolton. Those from Cartwright's weighed 23 drams. The weight of the shot would not be affected by passing through the bone, although in his opinion, passing through the frontal lobe would affect the shape.

William Simms

He was a collier and was going over Horwich Moor and called at Five Houses, and as he was leaving the beer-house, he met a Scotsman coming in about 10.00a.m. Going up the road, he met James Whittle between the Stumps and the Tunnel. He was carrying a gun, and he stopped and talked to him for about two or three minutes. He then went on to the Tunnel and the Cabin. There was nobody in the Cabin when he arrived. After a minute or two, an old tramp entered followed by Whittle about ten minutes later. Whittle did not have a gun with him. He left Whittle and the tramp together in the Cabin. He had been on the moor going to see his sister who lived in Belmont. The previous day he had been at work in Aspull at Lord Balcarres's mines. He had been two or three days idle and had spent his time with people about the pits. He had received 23 or 24 shillings the previous Saturday in wages. He had worked that week for Mr. Gray, Lord Balcarres's agent, but had been turned off for drinking. On that Friday, he had been to Mr. Orrel's factory at Belmont, and it was between 10.00 and 12.00 noon when he arrived there. He had dinner with his sister in Belmont and then went to shelter from the rain in the Cabin.

Daniel Cook

He was Constable of Sharples, and stated that on the Saturday following the killing, he went to arrest the prisoner. Whittle was brought out to him by Mr. Steward, Manager of the colliery, and he told Whittle that he was their prisoner. Whittle asked why this was happening, but Cook did not reply but brought out his handcuffs, however Whittle said he would go without them. Mr. Peter Ainsworth who was a magistrate, accompanied Cook to make the arrest, and Whittle was cautioned and told that he had no need to make a statement, but if he did, it could be used in evidence. Whittle said that he had not had a gun in the house since Sunday last. The whole party then set off to go to the Horwich constable. Cook and the prisoner walked together to Horwich and Robert Makin, Constable of Halliwell, walked behind them. Whilst walking, Whittle told Cook that he was innocent of this crime. Cook replied, "Jem, hadn't thee a gun in thy hands all yesterday?" Whittle replied, "No, not until the afternoon when I was with Matthew Lambert, and I shot a blue-beak, and I told him that the fellow that shot the Scotsman ought to suffer".

Robert Makin

He was Constable of Halliwell who stated that Whittle had told him that he had seen the Scotsman and had in fact spoken to him at Garbutt's stable door. Whittle had also told him that the dead man was not the first Scotsman who had gone up the road that day. There had been another and he had seen them both. Measurements were taken at the scene of the killing. The distance from Garbutt's house to the first coal pit at which James Fletcher worked was 420 yards, and the second pit was 55 yards from that. The distance from the furthest pit to where the body was found was 507 yards. The distance from where the body was found to the Cabin of the Tunnel was 309 yards. It was 220 yards from the stone delph to the Stumps through which the road went. The distance from the Stumps to the Tunnel was 137 yards, and it was 112 yards from the place where Fletcher heard the report of a gun.

James Corless

He was gamekeeper employed by Mr. Peter Ainsworth of Smithills Hall. He had been out on Horwich Moor with a shooting party consisting of Messrs Wright, Crompton, Ryding, Ireland, Horrocks and Ince. They were not local men but shooting guests of Mr. Ainsworth. He heard a gun fired on Smithills Moor about ½ mile from where the body was found. About five minutes later from a different direction, he heard another shot. The first shot was heard about 11.55a.m. and the second about noon. He was sure of the time because he had heard a factory bell ringing. The shots were not fired from his party because all the guns were close together the whole day because of the mist.

Address for the Defence – Mr Wilkins

"Members of the Jury, had it been made clear in your minds that the unfortunate man had in fact been murdered? After a good deal of investigation, I see good grounds for doubting this. Generally speaking, vindictiveness or a desire for gain are the incentives for murder. Was there any proof of vindictiveness on the part of my client towards the victim? Was there in fact, anything to warrant such a surmise? Was there any proof of a desire for gain? When the man was found, no money had been taken from him. His pack had not been disturbed, his stick and umbrella left untouched. The weather was very foggy, and it was such a time that poachers would carry out their operations. It seems possible and probable from the state of the deceased's dress that he had ventured to the roadside for some particular purpose, to answer a call of nature, and had been shot by some poacher ignorant to this day of the accident or knowing it, concealing that knowledge through fear of the consequences. Would this be a natural or forced surmise?

You have been asked to infer from the flesh near the wound, that the gun was near when the shot was fired, but anyone would know that discolouration would be produced around a wound by the blow of a gunshot from whatever distance the gun might have been fired. It was the custom of parties of Scotsmen in the neighbourhood to get their silver changed into notes at the beer-house. The victim Henderson called there and had paid for a glass of ale from his waistcoat pocket in which money was found after he had been discovered in the ditch. He did not ask for change, the presumption being that he had been unsuccessful in his collection on that day. There are reasonable doubts and they must be given to the accused. Suppose it was murder, then the question is who had committed the murder? The indictment points to the prisoner but what was the evidence? The testimony of Halliwell is utterly unworthy of belief and it is totally improbable that he had, by any honest means, become the owner of the property he stated he had in his possession on the day of the murder. This is borne out by his wholly unacceptable manner in which he has given his evidence, and as such, it should be regarded as defective. There is no continuity in the events he recalls, and there are gaps in his evidence which are unaccounted for. Elsewhere, there is not a point in the case which is not accounted for.

The prisoner was out shooting all day, but was this an uncommon circumstance? It was nothing more than usual or ordinary. From the coal-pit to Belmont there was not another single dwelling but one solitary Cabin. Knowing the area as he did and the habits of the Scotsmen, was not the circumstances that the man was killed so near his own home, rather an argument in favour of my client's innocence than guilt? It was given in evidence that he was a young man of mild temper with no blemishes on his character. This must also weigh well in his favour. I would ask you to consider whether or not there is sufficient evidence to support the view that there is proneness to fit and fashion facts to a particular set of circumstances? Looking at the testimony of Benjamin Burrell, it is quite clear that he had no apprehension when he turned around and saw the gun pointing at him, then the prisoner dropped it to his hip. He had no suspicion that he intended to fire at him. If indeed, he intended to murder him, he could have done so without having his back to him. Would not any person preparing to shoot at game, have dropped his gun to the rest on being spoken to? In fact, there is nothing more common than carrying a gun pointing, on shooting at moor game on a foggy day. I would ask you to consider if there was anything suspicious about the manner of the prisoner? He was without excitement when he came from his dinner and spoke to the carrier about the horse being ill. Mr. Garbutt had considered it rather extraordinary that he should have asked had he a horse ill. Why should this be so? It was an ordinary circumstance because he had a horse ill very often. He had one ill that day and the prisoner was a near neighbour. He was in no agitation, no trouble, no apprehension, and yet he walked about with an instrument of death in his hand. You have heard the testimony that my client did say at Matthew Lambert's, that he would have no more to do with shooting, but that arose from the annoyance from which he had been subjected by complaints from his father. Consider, if you will, the very important fact that the shots found in the brain of the deceased, were of uniform weight, while those in the shot bags and those in the box taken from the loaded gun were of different sizes. Those found in the gun and bag did not tally with those from the brain of the deceased. Members of the Jury, it is dangerous to lay too much emphasis on statements made by a person when apprehended, especially in a sudden manner. I therefore respectfully suggest that when my client had been questioned by the constable in the presence of his employer and local magistrate Mr. Ainsworth, and Mr. Wright, both of them owners of parts of the moor, he did in fact suspect that they intended to arrest him for poaching, and therefore made false statements to avoid being charged with that offence.

No witnesses being called for the Defence, Mr. Wilkins concluded his address to the Jury. The learned judge emphatically recapitulated all the leading points in the case, directing the Jury to give the prisoner the benefit of any doubts they might entertain. His Lordship dwelt particularly on the fact of all the shot found in the head of the deceased being of one size, whilst those which the prisoner had used proved to be of different sizes. The Jury retired at 9.00p.m. to consider the evidence and returned at 11.00p.m. with a verdict of NOT GUILTY. The Foreman of the Jury remarked that the decision had been arrived at in consequence of the defective evidence of Joseph Halliwell. James Whittle was immediately discharged.

The trial opened at 9.00a.m. in Liverpool Crown Court on Tuesday 2nd April 1839 and continued until 7.00p.m. Wilkins had succeeded in weakening the evidence of two or three material witnesses through stringent cross-examination. There was an adjournment of the court for thirty minutes for the defence to decide whether to call witnesses or proceed straight away to addressing the Jury. The latter course of action was taken with Mr. Wilkins surpassing himself by his speech to the Jury. He opened with his cool, quiet, deep sonorous voice, low but impressive and solemn, gaining the calm attention of the Jury to his remarks, proceeding step by step to unravel the facts, and urge upon the Jury such points as he considered important to the prisoner's case. He appealed so to the feelings and consciences of the Jury that the whole court was hushed, and pale stillness seemed to paralyse the whole audience there.

The cattle-dealer, Halliwell, overstated his evidence to the extent that Mr. Wilkins was able to shake his testimony and raise a doubt in the minds of the Jury, which lead them to believe that Halliwell was lying on oath. He also dwelt on other circumstances, the unimpeachable character of the prisoner's previous life, and the uncertainty and doubtfulness of relying solely on circumstantial evidence. Mr. Wilkins also raised the possibility that some sportsmen on the moor may have fired in the mist a chance shot without seeing or intending to harm anyone. The Jury returned a verdict at 11.00p.m.

When Whittle's father now aged between 60 and 70 went into the dock, they could be seen embracing each other.

A rare, personal account of the Trial proceedings is recorded in the autobiography of John Taylor, Attorney-at- Law of Bolton, which was published by the *Daily Chronicle* in 1883. Taylor opens his account by stating that during February and March of 1839, he was engaged in preparing the defence papers of James Whittle who had been charged with 'Wilful Murder', the case causing great excitement in the local neighbourhood. He makes the very important observation that the evidence for the prosecution was entirely circumstantial!

The defendant is described as a collier employed by Peter Ainsworth of Smithill Hall, Bolton. Whittle had an irreproachable character up to the time of the event. It appears that Whittle's friends who had promised him their support and help with the costs of the defence, failed to respond at the last minute. Ironically but perhaps not surprising, the Prosecution case was conducted regardless of cost.

Taylor retained as Whittle's Counsel, Charles Wilkins, later Sergeant Wilkins, a young barrister on the Northern Circuit who was regarded as one of the most eloquent counsel in England at the time. There is evidence that Taylor was undecided whether to abandon or proceed with the defence - the sum of £50 being necessary for legal costs but was not forthcoming. However, an arrangement was made between Taylor and Mr. Wilkins, whereby he was to be paid £5 to hold the brief, with the promise of further fees should they become available. It appears that for a period of twelve months, Mr. Taylor had no contact with the Whittle family, but on sending a promissory note for the outstanding fee of £50 for defence costs, the note was duly returned signed by Whittle and his father. It was agreed to pay the amount by monthly instalments, bearing in mind that the two parties were only labourers. Taylor concludes his account by stating that he was thankful to recover the costs within five years of the trial, receiving the total sum of £48. This result was proof that the Whittle family had a lasting remembrance of the services of their young attorney.

Chapter Three

A Re-assessment of the Case

In this final chapter, my aim is to present readers with an overview of the case in order to enable them to draw their own conclusions based upon an examination of the available evidence. In effect, I am placing the reader in the position of that of a potential juror.

By way of conclusion, I suggest several hypotheses which the reader may wish to consider in deciding whether or not the only suspect in this tragic case was in fact innocent or guilty. The re-assessment of the case commences with an examination of the known movements of the two principal players in the case; the victim George Henderson and the suspect James Whittle. The main sources of information are those provided by contemporary press reports of the incident. There are obvious limitations inherent in these sources, the main ones being repetition, sequential errors and of course, journalistic bias. However, as a counter-balance to these limitations, we are fortunate in having as an independent source, the account of both the preparation of Whittle's defence and the subsequent trial, in the autobiography of John Taylor, Whittle's attorney.

Henderson's Known Movements

The actual route taken by Henderson on the Friday morning from Blackrod is somewhat speculative, but there was a well-known track leading down from Blackrod towards Horwich passing through Anderton Hall Farm. This track continued through the area of Horwich known locally as Old Lord's Heights. This track emerged onto the Pike Road near to what was originally the Sportsman's Arms. This was built round 1817 to cater for sportsmen who came shooting on the moors. The inn was finally demolished in 1920 and replaced by a large cottage known locally as "Pike Cottage". The track continues alongside the cottage onto the moor and runs very close to Two Lads Cairn, eventually emerging onto the main Winter Hill road.

The first reference we have concerning Henderson's movement is from a Thomas Rutterworth, a fellow packman living in Blackrod. He had observed Henderson on the Thursday evening at the Old Cock Inn at Blackrod where he had stayed the night. He saw him leave the inn at approximately 8.00a.m. on his journey in the general direction of Horwich. The last known reference to Henderson is when he arrived at Garbutt's beer-house at about 12.00 noon. He did not stay there long before making his way up towards the summit of Winter Hill on his way to Belmont.

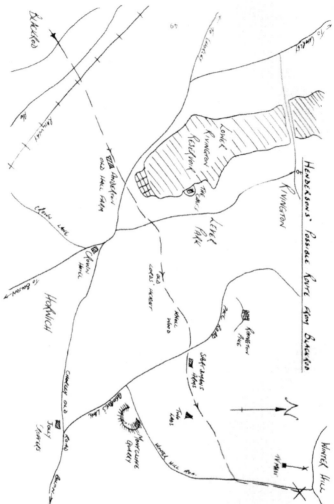

Map of Henderson's Possible Route from Blackrod.

Whittle's Known Movements

8.30a.m.	Between Garbutt's and Entwistle Lane with gun.
9.10a.m.	In the vicinity of Garbutt's with gun.
10.30a.m.	Between the Stumps and Winter Hill Tunnel with gun.
11.00a.m.	In the Cabin at Winter Hill Tunnel with gun.
11.30a.m.	Between a coal-pit and Five Houses with gun.
12.00 noon.	Seen coming from the summit of Winter Hill.
12.20p.m.	Seen coming from the direction of Horwich.
1.30p.m.	Arrived at Horwich Moorgate Inn with gun and shot birds.
4.00p.m.	Left Moorgate Inn with Matthew Lambert.
5.00p.m.	Seen outside Garbutt's without a gun.

The most obvious factor emerging from the known movements of Whittle, is his presence on the moors with a gun on the Friday morning. He was seen by witnesses on no less than five occasions. These occasions, viewed independently, would not arouse much interest, but taken collectively, provide sufficient evidence for Whittle to be considered a prime suspect for the shooting. Living in a scientific age as we do, it is easy to forget just how far scientific knowledge has progressed, particularly in the field of forensic science. It is difficult to fully appreciate the limitations imposed on those responsible for the investigation and detection of crime in the nineteenth century. At the time of the incident (1838), forensic medicine and the specialist field of ballistics were virtually unknown sciences. With the exception of the most obvious causes of death from crime, medical opinion rested on assumptions and hypotheses, rather than hard facts. In reviewing the aspects of this case, it would seem a fitting tribute to the progress of forensic detection to consider the various strands of our case, by utilising well-established and proven principles of forensic science as they apply to deaths due to firearms. Many of the sporting guns of the eighteenth and nineteenth centuries were of the flintlock type which, although popular with sportsmen, had the disadvantage of being slow in firing. When they were fired, the flash and smoke from the priming pan often temporarily obscured the target. There was also a perceptible time lag between the ignition of the primer and the explosion of the main charge.

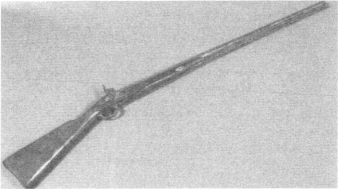

19th Century Percussion Lock Fowling Piece (see page 2)

In 1807, a Scottish clergyman, Alexander Forsyth, patented a lock which utilised the detonating powders of fulminating powder to ignite the charges in the barrel. This led to the conversion of flint-locks into percussion locks, in which a small amount of fulminate was detonated by a hammer and the flash directed into a touch hole. This method became recognised as the safest and most reliable free form of percussion ignition. From the first quarter of the nineteenth century onwards, most of the fowling pieces used for sports purposes would be the single barrel percussion type, using a mixture of lead shot. According to *Thornhill's Shooting Directory* of 1804, a mixture of No 1 and No 2 shot would comprise approximately 730 pellets per charge. The length of the average rifle barrel would be between 19½ and 39 inches, discounting the stock. From this information, we can assume that the fowling piece used by Whittle for shooting game on the day in question, was of a similar type in make to that shown above.

Gunshot wounds can be classified into three distinct groups; *contact, near contact and distant discharge.* A contact wound will appear split, scorched and possibly slightly blackened. In contrast, a near contact, usually defined as over six inches in distance, will only show a split entry wound and some scattering or tattooing with powder marks. A distant discharge, defined as anything from two to three feet from the body, will remain the same up to some 200 yards, then a split entry hole. The effective range of a sporting gun is approximately 50 yards or metres. The characteristic of a contact injury is that the shot will enter the body as a solid mass so the entry wound will approximate to the bore of the barrel. If the target is the head, the skull may be literally blown apart. Shot in its diffuse form, as fired from a distance, has little penetrating power. This means that exit wounds are not a feature of shotgun injuries other than in the contact situation. The maximum distance to which powder patches can be discharged depends on the barrel-length, the nature of the shot, and the powder load. At a range of as little as two or three yards, the entry-wound may show pellet holes. For ranges greater than this, the spread in inches may be taken as a rough guide to be equal to the distance in yards.

The pathological evidence as to the distance from which a shot has been fired can be deduced from the distinct group of gunshot wounds. A contact injury will show bruising due to the recoil of the gun - and a reproduction of the barrel may also be found on the skin. At very close range, unburnt powder will be discharged into the surrounding skin, leading to what is termed 'tattooing'. These effects will be diminished as the distance of the muzzle to wound increases. The critical distance is at about 2 yards, after which the shot begins to fan out, creating a pattern of entry in clothing and on the skin. A simple rule of thumb is that the diameter of the shot pattern in centimetres is approximately 2.5 to 3 times the muzzle distance from the wound in metres (or the spread in inches is equivalent to the distance in yards. The majority of shotgun injuries are overwhelmingly at close range. Certain features are strongly indicative of homicide (murder); a single wound of contact or very close range in an inaccessible position such as head or face is obvious. Contact and close-range entry wounds, bruising, blast effects, soot deposition and tattooing are all evident.

The direction of fire of a shotgun can only be determined from the entrance wound in close-range injuries. Shot spread over 20 inches will have been fired from a range of about 20 yards. When a shotgun is fired, the pellets begin to disperse soon after leaving the weapon. At close range (up to 3 feet), the shot will enter the body in a single mass, with the resultant large lacerated wound accompanied by burning and blackening. If a shot is fired at close range through the head, the skull will disintegrate with the shot exiting via openings such as the orbits or eye sockets.

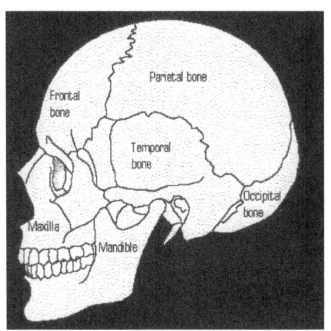

Bones of the Human Skull.

The Bones of the Human Skull

As suggested by Defence Counsel, it may have been in response to a call of nature that Henderson ventured off the road and into the ditch at the side. This would have placed him at a lower level than the adjoining moorland. If the shot was fired from the edge of the moor into the ditch at a range of less than three feet from the body, the shot through the temple would be at an angle. This would certainly place the killer less than a few feet away from the victim, certainly clear enough to see what he or she was doing. The Frontal and Occipital bones of the skull are the thickest, whilst the Temporal bones are much thinner and more susceptible to fracture. The medical evidence does suggest that most of the shot escaped through the left eye socket or orbit, which is certainly indicative of very close contact. The references to pieces of the victim's skull being found in the road adds further support to this theory. If Henderson had been shot whilst on the road, his body would have been propelled off the road by the force of the blast to the opposite side to where he was discovered.

There were no obvious signs to indicate this, or marks to suggest that the body had been dragged from the road to the ditch. This medical evidence rules out the possibility that the victim had strayed into the line of fire from either poachers or other sportsmen shooting on the moor. The only conclusion to be drawn from the medical evidence is that Henderson was the victim of a deliberate shooting. Looking back at the movements of the prime suspect, James Whittle, these timings if taken to be accurate, certainly place Whittle in the vicinity of the shooting at the material time. However, careful analysis of these timings does cast sufficient doubt that Whittle was, in fact, the perpetrator of the crime. The critical time frame on the day in question was between 12.00 noon and 12.30p.m. We are told that Whittle was seen passing Garbutt's beer-house at approximately 12.00 noon, going in the general direction of Winter Hill summit. However, this contradicts the statement of William Fletcher who had in fact accompanied Whittle back down the road on his way home at around 11.15a.m. This raises the obvious question: why would Whittle be going back up the road having already just come down it not less than three-quarters of an hour earlier?

By employing a few basic mathematical equations, it becomes quite evident that, given these timings, it would have been virtually impossible for Whittle to have committed the crime and be back at Garbutt's, all within a very tight time-frame. The measured distance from Five Houses or Garbutt's to the spot where Henderson's body was found was given as 972 yards. Assuming Whittle was walking uphill at a brisk pace, allowing for the fact that he was carrying a gun, and the weather was very misty, he could not have been walking at more than about three miles an hour. To reach the area of the shooting before Henderson arrived, it would have taken Whittle approximately 32 minutes, or if walking at say four miles an hour, at least 24 minutes. This would have placed Whittle at the scene at either 12.24 or 12.32p.m. If we assume Henderson, having arrived at Garbutt's beer-house at approximately 12.00 noon, and having drunk a glass of beer, it seems clear he could not have left before 12.05 or 12.10p.m. - at the earliest. Witnesses testified to having seen Whittle coming from his cottage at Five Houses with a gun and going in the direction of the Moorgate Inn at

Horwich at 12.20p.m. This being the case, he could not possibly have been at the scene of the shooting at the time it was estimated to have occurred. In the unlikely scenario that Whittle, having passed the beer-house whilst Henderson was still inside at 12.00 noon, having virtually run up the hill at a speed of say seven miles an hour, he could not have completed this round trip in less than 28 minutes. This theory is also strengthened by the statements of several witnesses who heard shots being fired around 12.30p.m.

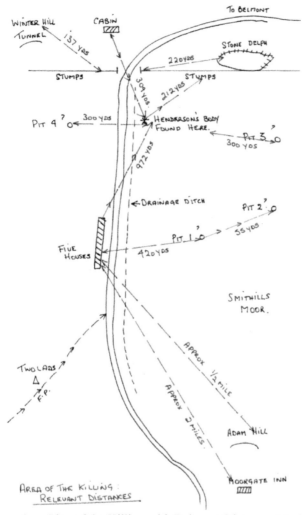

To BELMONT

WINTER HILL
TUNNEL
CABIN
137 YDS
STONE DELPH
220 YDS
STUMPS
STUMPS
308 YDS
212 YDS
PIT 4 ? O
300 YDS
HENDERSON'S BODY
FOUND HERE.
PIT 3 ? O
300 YDS
972 YDS
←DRAINAGE DITCH
PIT 2 ? O
FIVE
HOUSES
PIT 1 ? O
55 YDS
420 YDS
SMITHILLS
MOOR.
APPROX ½ MILE
TWO LADS
△
F.P.
APPROX 2 MILES.
ADAM HILL
AREA OF THE KILLING :
RELEVANT DISTANCES
MOORGATE INN

Area Plan of the Killing with Relevant Distances Marked.

The most damaging statement against Whittle came from Henderson's colleague Benjamin Burrell, who vividly describes his encounter with a man he believed to be Whittle. When this was recalled by the authorities, it is not difficult to see how the evidence was being stacked up against Whittle. Burrell was certain of the man's dress, height and even speech, which he described as being very similar to that of Whittle. However, one crucial piece of evidence is missing. Nowhere is there any reference made concerning the presence or absence of blood or powder stains on Whittle's clothing. Given the medical evidence of the extent of Henderson's injuries, it would be virtually impossible for the perpetrator not to have had some contact residue on their clothing. Whittle made no attempt to change his clothing before going to the Moorgate Inn later in the afternoon. These are hardly the actions of someone who had committed a murder. He was seen by several witnesses, none of whom made any reference to the state of his clothing, or to the presence of blood or powder staining. This, taken together with the timings of Whittle's movements, does cast doubt on him being the murderer.

At this stage in our re-assessment of the case, let us endeavour to place ourselves in the position of the potential killer, and consider the various options open to him or her. Given that the motive for the killing was considered to be robbery, this would presuppose that the killer or killers had prior knowledge of their victim and his movements. This would rule out the possibility of it being a chance or opportunist offence and would suggest a planned attack on a known victim presumed to have been carrying the objects of the attack, namely money and goods. The route of the potential victim being known in advance, the perpetrator or perpetrators would ensure that they were in the area ahead of the victim. The weather was misty and ideal for such an attack, and those responsible could avoid the possibility of being observed both before and after the attack. It would not be beyond the realms of possibility for such a plan to be carried out by persons living in the immediate area, whose chances of success far outweighed the risks of being apprehended in the act. The victim's movements for that particular Friday were well-known in the area, and an isolated spot was chosen for minimal disturbance and an escape route out onto the mist-covered moorlands. Having created for our purpose this hypothetical scenario, let us place the prime suspect Whittle into it, and see if any patterns emerge.

Whittle did have knowledge of the movements of the packmen, and of their purpose in calling at Garbutt's beer-house on their way home over Winter Hill, although he was not alone in this. However, unlike a well-planned robbery, Whittle appears to have made no attempt to disguise the fact that he was out shooting on the moors for most of the morning in question. He lived in the immediate area of the shooting, was well-known by neighbours and local mine workers for his habit of poaching - and appears to have been completely indifferent as to whether he was observed or not. These are hardly the actions of someone intent on carrying out an armed robbery. On reviewing the available evidence, one cannot help but conclude that Whittle's eventual arrest and charge was based entirely upon circumstantial evidence. Such evidence allows a conclusion to be drawn from a set of circumstances or information. In our case, several witnesses had testified to having seen Whittle with a gun at the material time. It may well be that these circumstances when viewed separately were insufficient to raise reasonable suspicion of Whittle's involvement, but when taken together, they quite likely created a strong suggestion of guilt.

In effect, this means that even though there may be only circumstantial evidence available, if there is enough of it taken as a whole, it may be sufficient to form the basis of a prosecution, which does appear to have happened in our case. His presence on the moor with a gun at the material time, provided those circumstances which lead the authorities to an inference of guilt, there being no direct evidence to link Whittle with either the victim or the crime scene itself. The traditional approach to circumstantial evidence has tended to be for the defence to underplay its significance, and for the prosecution to overplay it. However, no Jury should convict unless it can be sure that the standard of proof, "guilt beyond reasonable doubt" has been fully satisfied. So far as circumstantial evidence is concerned, any inference of guilt must be unequivocal and inexorable. The circumstances must point in one direction only. In effect, most of the evidence in criminal cases tends to be circumstantial, and rarely is there direct evidence of a criminal act. Having said this, it is sometimes regarded as of higher probative value than direct evidence, which does appear to have occurred in our specific case.

The prosecution suffered a serious setback with the defective evidence of the cattle-dealer Joseph Halliwell. It is surprising that his testimony was even considered admissible, and today he would certainly be considered an 'hostile witness'. His testimony was inconsistent and lacked clarity or comprehension, so it could not be taken as reliable in any sense, and even borders on perjury. What is more remarkable is the statement of William Stott, which does appear to have gone unchallenged by both the defence counsel or the Judge. The very fact that he had been approached by a certain party and urged to keep to his description of Whittle's clothing should have set alarm bells ringing very loudly. This is entirely consistent with a conspiracy to implicate Whittle, especially in view of the fact that there was a £100 reward on offer. It does appear to have been an abuse of process that Stott was not compelled on oath to furnish details of this approach and to identify the individual.

Whittle does make an incriminating statement to the constable on his being arrested. In this he describes the method by which Henderson had met his death - when he stated that he was shot with slugs or shot rather than with a bullet. This raises the question of how Whittle knew the cause of death despite not having viewed the body lying at Garbutt's. However, Whittle, being an experienced sportsman would be well aware that the usual method of shooting game was with shots or slugs and not bullets. Whittle did not own a gun and appears to have borrowed one from Mr Lambert, the landlord of the Moorgate Inn. His wife stated that her husband had lost a gun some time previous to the incident, and when this was mentioned to Whittle, he denied any knowledge of this gun. One could speculate that it was possible that Whittle had in fact, two guns in his possession on the day in question - one borrowed from Lambert, the other being the 'lost' gun. Whittle could then have committed the crime with the lost gun, then disposed of it, leaving him with just the one borrowed gun in his possession. This would ensure that when Henderson's post-mortem was carried out, the shot discovered in the victim's head would not correspond with that used in the borrowed gun.

Regarding a possible motive for the shooting, everything points towards robbery. We have the evidence of the victim's own words, "They have robbed me". Henderson's pockets were turned inside out, and very little money was found on the body. However, the pack he was carrying had not been disturbed and the contents were still intact. This would be expected if robbery was the motive, when a search of the victim's belongings would have occurred for anything of value. There is also the fact that Henderson's employer, Mr. Jardine, surmised that he would not have had in his possession more than about £15 in money on that Friday.

Turning briefly from Whittle as the main suspect in the case, there are a number of alternative theories that the reader may wish to consider. There is the possibility that some person or persons followed Henderson that morning from Blackrod, having possibly been customers at the Old Cock Inn the previous evening. Henderson's movements would be well known by many of the locals because of his regular habit of travelling a particular area. One witness at the Inquest testified to having seen Henderson pay for drinks with silver on the Thursday evening, and no doubt others present would have witnessed this.

The theory that Henderson may have been followed, rests on the presumption that he would stop off along his route home to receive collections of money. By the time he reached Garbutt's beer-house, he would have completed his rounds and presumably have substantial takings in his possession. Any person or persons contemplating robbery would almost certainly choose an isolated spot along the route to carry out the deed, and Winter Hill would be that ideal spot. The weather on the Friday morning provided the ideal cover for such an attempt. There are several alternative tracks over the moor. These would make it easier for those contemplating such an attempt to have arrived ahead of Henderson and be unseen by any witnesses. As for the shooting itself, there is the possibility that he was shot out of frustration by the perpetrators having found that he had in fact, not made any collections that morning - and they could not risk being identified by Henderson.

Our sources give very few details concerning the tramp seen with Whittle in the Cabin at the Winter Hill Tunnel prior to the shooting. It appears that there was no effort made to trace him as a possible witness. There is also the shooting party from Smithills Hall who were seen out on the moor at the material time. We are informed by Corless, the gamekeeper, that the party had stayed close together because of the mist.

There are no references made to the type of guns being used by this party having been taken in for examination. This could very well have been as a result of their host Peter Ainsworth, a local magistrate, landowner and employer being considered beyond suspicion. Whittle was a known poacher and had, no doubt, incurred the wrath of the local gamekeepers. Even if the fatal shot was fired from one of the shooting party, it would have been regarded as accidental, because the party would not have ventured within distance of the known road over Winter Hill. Once it had been established that Whittle was out on the moors with a gun, this would have provided an ideal scapegoat for the crime. We are, therefore, left with two possible conclusions, notwithstanding the important fact that Whittle was finally acquitted of the crime.

Firstly, if Whittle had indeed been the perpetrator of the crime, he had not taken any effective steps to conceal his movements on the day in question – in fact, quite the opposite. As pointed out by his defence counsel, Whittle lived at Five Houses and was well-known in the area, and this would have made him the prime suspect. When arrested, Whittle did make several statements which on reflection, could be regarded as self-incriminating. Why such statements were made - possibly out of fear or apprehension - remains unclear. The second possibility can be deduced from the evidence of witnesses. It does appear that Whittle was presented very much as a victim of circumstances, being in the wrong place at the wrong time. What is revealing is that at the Inquest, there was not a single witness who came forward to support Whittle. What is equally significant is the fact that the defence was conducted without ever calling witnesses, this being a most unusual procedure. This would suggest reluctance on the part of local people to come forward in Whittle's defence possibly for fear for their own livelihoods. There could be a more sinister reason - that of wishing to shield some other guilty party by providing a conspiracy of silence.

Finally, there is the role of the 'mystery' woman. The press reports of the Inquest in the *Blackburn Standard* refer to Whittle's clandestine relationship with a young woman in the neighbourhood. Other details are not forthcoming, and she was never called by either the defence or prosecution as a witness at the Inquest or Trial. This does appear to be rather strange given that Whittle intended to marry her that same month. This situation suggests that Whittle may not have been the only suitor for this woman, and certainly strengthens a conspiracy theory. Finally, there is also the possibility, however exaggerated, that Henderson himself may have struck up a friendship with the woman during his travels and Whittle, or someone else, had found this out and decided to seek revenge. However, these suggestions are purely speculative.

After Whittle's acquittal, the person or persons responsible for the brutal killing were never found, so the mystery is perpetuated by the passage of time. Whittle was true to his word and never went shooting again after the trial. In fact he went blind prior to his death. To those who were convinced of his guilt, this was seen as a sign of how close he had come to the gallows.

The burial register in Horwich Parish Church shows an entry for James Whittle, who died on April 16th, 1871, at the age of 55 years. The spot where Henderson met his death was originally marked by a small tree which over the years was gradually stripped by souvenir hunters. The site is now marked by a single old water-pipe erected in 1912. The site is known locally as "Scotchman's Stump".

Sadly, we shall never know the truth behind this tragic murder of George Henderson as the secret died with him.

Sources

The main sources consulted in this work were:

Primary Sources

'Autobiography of John Taylor of Bolton,' edited by
James Clegg, Bolton, 1883.
Blackburn Standard, November, 1838.
Bolton Chronicle, November, 1838.
Hampson's History of Horwich, 1883.
Liverpool Mercury, April, 1839.
Manchester Courier, November, 1838.
Preston Chronicle, April, 1839.

Secondary Sources

Garrett, G & Nott, A, *Cause of Death,* Robinson,
London, 2001.
Knight, B, *Simpson's Forensic Medicine,* Edward
Arnold, London, 1991.
Simpson, K. *Forty Years of Murder,* London, 1978.
Simpson, K. & Knight, B. *Forensic Medicine,*
London, 1985.
Stern, C. *Iain West's Casebook,* Little Brown,
London, 1996.
*Taylor's Principles and Practice of Medical
Jurisprudence,* 13th edition, London, 1984.

Photographs and Sketch Maps

All the photographs and sketches produced are by the
author.
The following Grid References may be of interest to
those readers wishing to visit the area of the crime.
They are based on the Ordnance Survey Map No 287
– West Pennine Moors:

Old Lords Heights	SD	64485 12665
Sportsman's Arms		64876 13164
Montcliffe Colliery		65406 12289
Site of Five Houses		65703 13589
Scotchman's Stump		66116 14541
The Stumps Boundary		66246 14672
Winter Hill Tunnel Site		66318 14689

Printed in Great Britain
by Amazon